Saint Peregrine

Novena and Prayers

By
Mary Mark Wickenhiser, FSP

Pauline
BOOKS & MEDIA
Boston

Nihil Obstat: Rev. Thomas W. Buckley

Imprimatur: ✠ Most Rev. Seán O'Malley, O.F.M.Cap.
Archbishop of Boston
January 19, 2004

ISBN 0-8198-7079-X

Cover art: Tom Kinarney

Texts of the New Testament used in this work are taken from *The St. Paul Catholic Edition of the New Testament,* translated by Mark A. Wauck. Copyright © 1992, Society of St. Paul. All rights reserved.

Texts of the Psalms used in this work are translated by Manuel Miguens. Copyright © 1995, Daughters of St. Paul.

"P" and PAULINE are registered trademarks of the Daughters of St. Paul

Printed and published in the U.S.A. by Pauline Books & Media, 50 Saint Pauls Avenue, Boston MA 02130-3491.

www.pauline.org

Pauline Books & Media is the publishing house of the Daughters of St. Paul, an international congregation of women religious serving the Church with the communications media.

2 3 4 5 6 7 8 9   12 11 10 09 08 07 06 05

Contents

What Is a Novena?

The Catholic tradition of praying novenas has its roots in the earliest days of the Church. In the Acts of the Apostles we read that after the ascension of Jesus, the apostles returned to Jerusalem, to the upper room, where "They all devoted themselves single-mindedly to prayer, along with some women and Mary the Mother of Jesus and his brothers" (Acts 1:14). Jesus had instructed his disciples to wait for the coming of the Holy Spirit, and on the day of Pentecost, the Spirit of the Lord came to them. This prayer of the first Christian community was the first "novena." Based on this, Christians have always prayed for various needs, trusting that God both hears and answers prayer.

The word "novena" is derived from the Latin term *novem*, meaning nine. In biblical times numbers held deep symbolism for people. The number "three," for example, symbolized perfection, fullness, completeness. The number nine—three times three—symbolized perfection times perfection. Novenas developed because it was thought that—symbolically speaking—nine days represented the perfect amount of time to pray. The ancient Greeks and Romans had the custom of mourning for nine days after a death. The early Christian Church offered Mass for the deceased for nine consecutive days. During the Middle Ages novenas in preparation for solemn feasts became popular, as did novenas to particular saints.

Whether a novena is made solemnly—in a parish church in preparation for a feastday—or in the privacy of one's home, as Christians we never really pray alone. Through the waters of Baptism we have become members of the Body of Christ and are thereby united to every other member of Christ's Mystical Body. When we pray, we are spiritually united with all the other members.

Just as we pray for each other while here on earth, those who have gone before us and are united with God in heaven can pray for us and intercede for us as well. We Catholics use the term "communion of saints" to refer to this exchange of spiritual help among the members of the Church on earth, those who have died and are being purified, and the saints in heaven.

While nothing can replace the celebration of Mass and the sacraments as the Church's highest form of prayer, devotions have a special place in

Catholic life. Devotions such as the Stations of the Cross can help us enter into the sufferings of Jesus and give us an understanding of his personal love for us. The mysteries of the rosary can draw us into meditating on the lives of Jesus and Mary. Devotions to the saints can help us witness to our faith and encourage us in our commitment to lead lives of holiness and service as they did.

How to use this booklet

The morning and evening prayers are modeled on the Liturgy of the Hours, following its pattern of psalms, scripture readings, and intercessions.

We suggest that during the novena you make time in your schedule to pray the morning prayer and evening prayer. If you are able, try to also set aside a time during the day when you can pray the novena and any other particular prayer(s) you have chosen. Or you can recite the devotional prayers at the conclusion of the morning or evening prayer. What is important is to pray with expectant faith and confidence in a loving God who will answer our prayers in the way that will most benefit us. The Lord "satisfies the thirsty, and the hungry he fills with good things" (Ps 107:9).

St. Peregrine

Patron of Cancer Patients

St. Peregrine, whose name means "pilgrim," was an Italian Servite who dedicated himself to the care of the sick and the poor. He worked tirelessly, spent long hours in prayer, and drew people to God. But that was after his conversion.

As a young man in the city of Forli, Peregrine had little concern for religion. He even actively took part in the anti-papal politics of his town. Because of discontent among the people, the pope sent Fr. Philip Benizi (who was also later canonized) to act as a mediator. The townspeople insulted and mistreated him, however, and Peregrine led a group of young men who attacked the priest and drove him from the city. Peregrine struck Fr. Benizi on the face, but the priest, literally following Jesus' words, only offered him the other cheek.

The look that Fr. Benizi gave Peregrine pierced the young man's heart—a look of compassion, love and pardon. Peregrine couldn't shake the impression it left on him, and it led him to a change of heart. He asked Fr. Philip's forgiveness, left aside his former way of life, and dedicated himself to prayer and solitude.

During this time he developed a trusting devotion to the Blessed Mother. On one occasion he felt Mary was speaking to him, urging him to join "her servants"—the Servites. Peregrine followed this call, and Fr. Philip received him into the Order.

Peregrine spent his life as a lay brother in the Servites, and he went to Forli to work among his own people. He did pastoral work in hospitals and prisons, and often visited the poor. He spent his days and nights visiting the sick and dying, comforting them by his presence, words, and actions.

A life of poverty and penance eventually left its mark on the aging Peregrine. A painful cancerous sore developed on his leg, and in order to save his life the doctors decided to amputate. Surgery was extremely painful and a great risk in those days. Dreading the thought of amputation and its aftermath, Peregrine spent the night before the operation in prayer. Taken up into a mystical state, he saw the figure of Jesus on the crucifix above him come down and touch the painful wound. Peregrine thought that he had been dreaming, but when he looked at his leg, the sore was gone. He was cured! The doctors testified that they could no longer detect any trace of the cancerous growth.

For this reason, St. Peregrine has been chosen the patron of all who suffer from any type of cancer. Having suffered from this disease, he understands the pain of those who are ill, and intercedes for them before God.

Marianne Lorraine Trouvé, FSP

Morning Prayer

Morning prayer is a time to give praise and thanks to God, to remind ourselves that he is the source of all beauty and goodness. Lifting one's heart and mind to God in the early hours of the day puts one's life into perspective: God is our loving Creator who watches over us with tenderness and is always ready to embrace us with his compassion and mercy.

While at prayer, try to create a prayerful atmosphere, perhaps with a burning candle to remind you that Christ is the light who illumines your daily path, an open Bible to remind you that the Lord is always present, a crucifix to remind you of the depths of God's love for you. Soft music can also contribute to a serene and prayerful mood.

If a quiet place is not available, or if you pray as you commute to and from work, remember that the God who loves you is present everywhere and hears your prayer no matter the setting.

It is good to give thanks and praise the Lord our
     God,
to proclaim his love in the morning.
Glory be to the Father, and to the Son, and to the
     Holy Spirit,
as it was in the beginning, is now, and will be
     forever. Amen.

———————⦿———————

Psalm 113

Praise the Lord our God who helps all those in need.

Praise, you servants of the LORD,
praise the name of the LORD.
May the name of the LORD be blessed
now, and forever more.
The name of the LORD is to be praised
from the rising of the sun to its setting.
The LORD is exalted over all the nations,
his splendor is above the heavens.
Who is like the LORD our God
who is enthroned on high,
who deigns to look down upon heaven and earth?
The LORD raises the poor from the dust,
lifts up the needy from the ash heap,
to give them a place among the princes,
among the rulers of his people.

To the barren woman God gives a home
and makes her the joyful mother of children.

Glory be to the Father...

The Word of God
Matthew 13:44–46

When we seek to understand its value, suffering can be the "hidden treasure" in our lives. It can be a gift given to God for the well-being of others and for the sake of God's kingdom here on earth. Suffering is that gift which can only be given by the one who suffers.

"The Kingdom of Heaven is like a treasure hidden in a field which a man found and hid, and in his joy he went off and sold all he had and bought that field.

"Again, the Kingdom of Heaven is like a merchant seeking fine pearls; when he found one very precious pearl he went and sold off all he had and bought it."

I hope in your words, I trust in your love.

*From prayer one draws the strength needed to
meet the challenges of daily life as a committed
follower of Jesus Christ and, as such, to be a living
sign of the Lord's loving presence in the world.*

Intercessions

Lord, I praise and thank you for the gift of a
new day, coming into your presence to seek
your grace and blessings:

Response: Lord, lead me in your love.

Grant that I may recognize your loving Providence at work in the events of this day. **R.**

Grant that by all I say and do, and by the pain I
experience today, others may be touched by your
love flowing through me. **R.**

Grant that I may spend this day in joy of spirit
and peace of mind, knowing that you are with me
in my pain. **R.**

Grant that all those I love may be kept from
harm this day. **R.**

(Add your own general intentions and your particular intentions for this novena.)

Conclude your intercessions by praying to our heavenly Father in the words Jesus taught us:

Our Father, who art in heaven, hallowed be thy name; thy kingdom come; thy will be done on earth as it is in heaven. Give us this day our daily bread, and forgive us our trespasses, as we forgive those who trespass against us, and lead us not into temptation, but deliver us from evil. Amen.

———— ❧ ————

Closing Prayer

Good and gracious God, open my heart to receive the blessings you want to pour out on me today. Keep me faithful to your love and free from all sin. I ask this through Jesus Christ, your Son. Amen.

Let us praise the Lord.
And give him thanks.

Novena to St. Peregrine

S t. Peregrine, you are called "the wonder worker" because of the countless miracles you obtain from God for those who ask your intercession. You responded to God's call with a ready spirit, dedicating your life to the service of others, exhausting your energies by ministering to the poor and oppressed in hospitals and prisons. Your great desire to enter into the sufferings of Jesus enabled you to accept a painful affliction with serene endurance until the touch of Jesus Crucified miraculously healed the incurable wound in your leg.

Holy Peregrine, obtain for me the grace to be attentive to what the Lord is asking of me at this time in my life and to respond with courage and faith in God's compassionate love for me. Enkindle in my heart a desire to unite my sufferings to those of Jesus and, for his love, to serve others who are in need. Trusting in the Lord's promise that whatever is asked in Jesus' name will be granted, I ask this particular grace (*mention your request*). I praise God for the many blessings I have already received from his generous love, and I look to the day when I can glorify him with all the saints in heaven. Amen.

———∞———

Our Father, who art in heaven, hallowed be they name; thy kingdom come; thy will be done on earth as it is in heaven. Give us this day our daily bread, and forgive us our trespasses, as we forgive those who trespass against us, and lead us not into temptation, but deliver us from evil. Amen.

———∞———

Hail Mary, full of grace, the Lord is with you. Blessed are you among women, and blessed is the fruit of your womb, Jesus. Holy Mary, Mother of God, pray for us sinners, now and at the hour of our death. Amen.

Glory be to the Father, and to the Son, and to the Holy Spirit, as it was in the beginning, is now, and will be forever. Amen.

St. Peregrine, pray for us.

Various Prayers

Prayer to Obtain a Special Favor

*G*ood and gracious God, you gave St. Peregrine an angel as his companion, the Mother of God as his teacher, and Jesus as his healer. Grant that I, too, may love and reverence my guardian angel; that I may love and venerate the Blessed Mother; that I may ever seek to praise and worship Jesus, my Savior, until I am with them in heaven for all eternity.

Compassionate Lord, giver of all good things, through the intercession of St. Peregrine, grant me the graces that you know I need most at this time, especially the favor I ask (*mention your request*). I ask this and all things through Christ, your Son. Amen.

(Our Father, Hail Mary, Glory be…)

St. Peregrine, pray for us.

Prayer for Healing

*G*od of goodness and mercy, I praise and thank you for the many blessings I have received through your generous love. Grant me the grace to be attentive to all you are asking of me at this time in my life and to respond with courage and faith in your compassionate love for me. Let me spend my life doing good and avoiding all that is not in accord with your will for me.

Trusting in your goodness, and with confidence in your power to heal, I humbly ask, through the intercession of St. Peregrine, for this grace *(mention your request)*. May all nations come to know the power of your love and the unfailing gift of your mercy so that one day we may glorify you with all the saints in heaven. Amen.

Prayer for Someone with Cancer

*A*lmighty and eternal God, healer of those who trust in you, through the intercession of St. Peregrine, hear my prayer for *(name)*. In your tender mercy, restore her/him to bodily health that she/he may give you thanks, praise your name, and proclaim your wondrous love to all. I ask this through Christ your Son, our Lord. Amen.

――――――※――――――

Prayer for the Family of a Cancer Patient

*C*ompassionate and loving God, among your many gifts, one most cherished is the love of family. I ask, now, that you be particularly mindful of _____'s family; hold each of them in your loving hands and care for them. Give them courage and patience, hope and optimism; relieve their fears and anxieties. During this difficult time, let your love sustain them, and their love for one another be a support and consolation. Amen.

St. Peregrine, pray for them.

――――――※――――――

Prayer of Praise and Thanksgiving

It is fitting for us to praise and thank God for the graces and privileges he has bestowed upon the saints. Devotees of St. Peregrine may pray the following act of thanksgiving during their novena.

*L*ord Jesus, I praise, glorify, and bless you for all the graces and privileges you have bestowed upon your chosen servant and pastor of souls, St. Peregrine. By his merits grant me your grace, and through his intercession help me in all my needs. At the hour of my death be with me until that time when I can join the saints in heaven to praise you forever and ever. Amen.

———————— ✥ ————————

Litany in Honor of St. Peregrine

(for private use)

Lord, have mercy on us.
Christ, have mercy on us.
Lord, have mercy on us.
Christ, hear us.
Christ, graciously hear us.

God, the Father of heaven, *have mercy on us.*
God, the Son, Redeemer of the world,
    have mercy on us.
God, the Holy Spirit, *have mercy on us.*
Holy Trinity, one God, *have mercy on us.*
Holy Mary, Mother of God, *pray for us.*
Mother of Sorrows, *pray for us.*
Health of the sick, *pray for us.*
Comforter of the afflicted, *pray for us.*
Help of Christians, *pray for us.*
St. Peregrine, *pray for us.*

You who suffered from a cancerous lesion,
pray for us.

You who were cured by the outstretched hand of
Jesus crucified, *pray for us*.

You who performed miracles in the name of Jesus,
pray for us.

You who cured the sick through the power of Jesus,
pray for us.

You who converted sinners through prayer and
fasting, *pray for us*.

You who receive every favor asked of God,
pray for us.

Peregrine, confident in prayer, *pray for us*.

Peregrine, austere in penance, *pray for us*.

Peregrine, patient in suffering, *pray for us*.

Peregrine, most humble servant of God,
pray for us.

Peregrine, ever zealous for souls, *pray for us*.

Peregrine, ever kind toward the afflicted,
pray for us.

You who were most devoted to the passion of Jesus
and the sorrows of Mary, *pray for us*.

You who offered your life for the salvation of souls,
pray for us.

You who work wonders for the sick and diseased,
pray for us.

You who give hope to those with incurable cancer,
pray for us.

Peregrine, universal patron of all who suffer from cancer, *pray for us.*

Peregrine, beloved patron of Spain, *pray for us.*

Peregrine, glory of the Order of the Servants of Mary, *pray for us.*

Lamb of God, you take away the sins of the world, *spare us, O Lord.*

Lamb of God, you take away the sins of the world, *graciously hear us, O Lord.*

Lamb of God, you take away the sins of the world, *have mercy on us.*

V. Pray for us, holy St. Peregrine,

R. That we may become worthy of the promises of Christ.

Let us pray.

O God, be gracious and hear the prayers which we present to you through the intercession of St. Peregrine, your dedicated servant. May we who trust in your faithfulness receive help in our time of need. We ask this through Christ, our Lord. Amen.

Evening Prayer

*A*s this day draws to a close, we place ourselves in an attitude of thanksgiving. We take time to express our gratitude to a loving God for his abiding presence. We thank him for the gift of the day and all it has brought with it. We thank him for all the things we were able to achieve throughout the day, and we entrust to him the concerns we have for tomorrow.

From the rising to the setting of the sun,
may the name of the Lord be praised.
Glory be to the Father, and to the Son, and to the
    Holy Spirit,
as it was in the beginning, is now, and will be
    forever. Amen.

Take a few moments for a brief examination of conscience. Reflect on the ways God acted in your life today, how you responded to his invitations to think, speak, and act in a more Christ-like manner, and in

*what ways you would like to be a more faithful disciple
tomorrow.*

Lord, in your great love have mercy.
For the times I lacked in compassion and concern
for others.
Lord, in your great love have mercy.
For the times I acted out of anger, jealously, or re-
venge.
Lord, in your great love have mercy.
For the times I was untruthful or unforgiving.
Lord, in your great love have mercy.
For the times… (any other petitions for pardon).

(Or any other Act of Sorrow)

Psalm 23

The Lord abides with us.

The LORD is my shepherd;
nothing do I want.
He makes me lie down in verdant pastures,
he guides me along soothing streams.
He refreshes my soul.
He leads me along paths of righteousness
for the sake of his name.
Even though I walk in the dark valley I fear no
     evil,

because you are with me.
Your rod and your staff give me courage.
You spread the table before me in the face of my
    foes;
you have anointed my head with oil;
my cup overflows.
May only contentment and loving kindness
be with me all the days of my life,
and may I dwell in the house of the LORD for years
    to come.

Glory be to the Father...

The Word of God
Matthew 11:28–30

*"Come to me...." A simple yet challenging way to
face life's problems. Jesus invites us to take refuge in
him, to allow him to rescue, restore, and renew us in
our daily journey back to the Father.*

"Come to me, all you grown weary and bur-
dened,
and I will refresh you.
Take my yoke upon you
and learn from me,
For I am gentle and humble hearted,
and you will find rest for your souls;

For my yoke is easy,
and my burden light."

I hope in your promise. I trust in your word.

———————⚭———————

In prayer we bring before the Lord our own needs and the needs of those we love. We take time to consider the needs of the world and intercede for those who do not or cannot pray. We offer petitions for the improvement of the human condition, so that our world will be a better place to live and all people may contribute to building up God's kingdom here on earth.

Intercessions

*G*od of compassion and love, we thank you for the gifts you have given us this day. With confidence in your loving care, we offer our needs and the needs of all humanity.

Response: Lord, hear our prayer through the intercession of St. Peregrine.

That all those who minister in your name may lead lives of holiness and seek to be true witnesses to the Gospel message of love and compassion, we pray. **R.**

That world leaders may govern with integrity and justice, safeguard the rights of all human persons, and provide for the needs of their people, especially the sick and disabled, we pray. **R.**

That those who suffer in body, mind, or spirit (*especially N.*) may know the healing touch of the Divine Master, we pray. **R.**

That those living in healthcare treatment facilities may experience the patience and compassion of committed and loving caregivers, we pray. **R.**

That those dedicated to medical research, and all those who work to eliminate or control disease, may open themselves to the Spirit's gifts of wisdom and good judgment, we pray. **R.**

That caregivers and hospice workers may know the joy and self-fulfillment that comes from serving others, we pray. **R.**

That those who are terminally ill (*especially N.*) may walk hand in hand with God to receive comfort and strength in their pain, fear, and anxiety, we pray. **R.**

That those who have died (*especially N.*) may soon enjoy light, happiness, and peace in the joy of heaven, we pray. **R.**

(Add your own general intentions and your particular intentions for this novena.)

Conclude your intercessions by praying to our heavenly Father in the words Jesus taught us:

Our Father, who art in heaven...

—————————❧—————————

Closing Prayer

*G*racious Lord, receive our evening prayer. Guard us from evil and bring us safely through the night, so that with the coming of a new day we may serve you more faithfully. We ask this through Christ, your Son, our Lord. Amen.

Mary, Jesus' Mother and ours, is always ready to intercede for those who ask her help.

Remember, O most gracious Virgin Mary, that never was it known that anyone who fled to your protection, implored your help or sought your intercession, was left unaided. Inspired with this confidence, I fly to you, O Virgin of virgins, my Mother; to you I come; before you I kneel, sinful and sorrowful. O Mother of the Word Incarnate, despise not my petitions, but in your mercy hear and answer me. Amen.

May God's blessing remain with us forever. In the name of the Father, and of the Son, and of the Holy Spirit. Amen.

BOOKS & MEDIA

The Daughters of St. Paul operate book and media centers at the following addresses. Visit, call or write the one nearest you today, or find us on the World Wide Web, www.pauline.org

CALIFORNIA

3908 Sepulveda Blvd, Culver City, CA 90230 310-397-8676

5945 Balboa Avenue, San Diego, CA 92111 858-565-9181

46 Geary Street, San Francisco, CA 94108 415-781-5180

FLORIDA

145 S.W. 107th Avenue, Miami, FL 33174 305-559-6715

HAWAII

1143 Bishop Street, Honolulu, HI 96813 808-521-2731

Neighbor Islands call: 866-521-2731

ILLINOIS

172 North Michigan Avenue, Chicago, IL 60601 312-346-4228

LOUISIANA

4403 Veterans Memorial Blvd, Metairie, LA 70006 504-887-7631

MASSACHUSETTS

885 Providence Hwy, Dedham, MA 02026 781-326-5385

MISSOURI

9804 Watson Road, St. Louis, MO 63126 314-965-3512

NEW JERSEY

561 U.S. Route 1, Wick Plaza, Edison, NJ 08817 732-572-1200

NEW YORK

150 East 52nd Street, New York, NY 10022 212-754-1110

PENNSYLVANIA

9171-A Roosevelt Blvd, Philadelphia, PA 19114 215-676-9494

SOUTH CAROLINA

243 King Street, Charleston, SC 29401 843-577-0175

TENNESSEE

4811 Poplar Avenue, Memphis, TN 38117 901-761-2987

TEXAS

114 Main Plaza, San Antonio, TX 78205 210-224-8101

VIRGINIA

1025 King Street, Alexandria, VA 22314 703-549-3806

CANADA

3022 Dufferin Street, Toronto, Ontario, Canada M6B 3T5 416-781-9131

¡También somos su fuente para libros, videos y música en español!